I0478841

BOOMER CASHOUT

INCREASE YOUR BUSINESS'S VALUE & MARKETABILITY TO SELL FOR RETIREMENT

WITH AFFORDABLE ONLINE TOOLS

LISA KIPPS-BROWN

Boomer Cashout: Increase Your Business's Value & Marketability to Sell For Retirement

Copyright © 2017 Lisa Kipps-Brown

Training Programs:
We offer training programs and workshops for groups and individuals, both online and live, in-person. If you're interested in learning more, contact information is below.

For more information about this title or about other training programs, contact the publisher:
Glerin Business Resources, Inc.
PO Box 295, Halifax, Virginia 24558
888-318-2795
Website: www.glerin.com
Email: info@glerin.com

Cover Design: Erin Kipps Brown

Kipps-Brown, Lisa
Boomer Cashout: Increase Your Business's Value & Marketability to Sell For Retirement
ISBN 978-1547031184

Dedicated to my husband, Tom.

Without you, I wouldn't be the person I am today.

Table of Contents

Preface

Boomer Cashout is the result of the crossroads of two of my passions: helping transform small businesses through smart use of the web, and helping Economic Developers support their local businesses to strengthen the economy.

Over the years I've noticed that too many Boomers aren't keeping up with the changes in technology that can help their businesses be more valuable and marketable to others, especially to younger buyers. It's hard enough to sell a business, but this technology gap is only making it harder.

I want you to be able to sell your business and enjoy the fruits of your labor! This book isn't meant to be in-depth instructions of what to do, but more to introduce you to new technologies and ways of thinking that can help you make your business more likely to sell. It's written in mostly layman's terms, assuming most of you don't know what a lot of the tech terms mean because I don't want to leave anyone behind.

For communities to be competitive in attracting new business prospects, it's critical that we keep more small businesses open from generation to generation.

Businesses like yours are what give our communities their unique local flavor and form the backbone of local economies.

My father owned a small music and appliance store when I was growing up. When he decided to retire due to health reasons, he closed the store, liquidated inventory, and sold the building. Decades later people in the community still approach me with fond memories and stories of how much his store meant to them. It wasn't just a store to those people. It was a part of their lives, and chances are your business is a part of many people's lives as well.

I couldn't help him keep his store open, but if I can help just one more small business be sold rather than closing down when the owner retires, I'll get the satisfaction of knowing an entire community benefits.

Thanks for reading!

The Boomer Technology Gap

Hey, Boomer! You've worked hard to build your business, and now you're starting to think about cashing out to enjoy your retirement years. Just think, for probably the first time ever you'll be able to do what you want when you want – play golf, lounge on the beach, have cocktails by the pool, travel the world, or just relax in your own back yard.

Not so fast, though!

According to Christopher M. Snider, President and CEO of the Exit Planning Institute (EPI), 85-90% of the net worth of the average business owner is tied up in their business, yet "57% of respondents to their survey stated that lifestyle is not dependent on transfer of ownership of the business." That's called denial.

Did you know that around 2/3 of small businesses never sell and are just closed when the owner retires? And of those that do sell, the average sales price is about 1/2 of what the owner thinks it's worth?

Combine the dismal sales figures with owners having the vast majority of their financial assets tied up in their businesses, and the prospects for the average owner to ever retire comfortably are slim. And it's getting even harder.

Your own technology gap can be a retirement trap.

"It's a different world now, and I know from my over 20 years of experience in the internet industry that most of you haven't changed with it."

What's the technology gap? It's the difference between how you use and interact with technology versus how Gen X, Gen Y, and Millennials do.

Boomers have the new hurdle of how drastically the web has changed the business world since most of us started our businesses. It's a different world now, and I know from my over 20 years of experience in the internet industry that most of you haven't changed with it.

You've been too busy running your business to even think about it, and that presents a big problem:

The generations following Boomers are more tech-savvy, expect businesses to be using technology, and don't want to buy a business that isn't positioned to be competitive for the future. They also don't want to buy a job, and incorporating technology wisely will help the business rely less on you for day-to-day operations.

The plethora of affordable, readily-available online tools that can streamline business means that today's buyers expect those tools to be integrated into your business. If they're not, the business is automatically worth much less. And if a buyer has to put too much work into modernizing your business, they may as well start one from scratch.

Think in terms of houses: an older home with an updated kitchen and bath will sell faster and for more than the same home with outdated décor, fixtures, and appliances. And at the bottom of the barrel is the fixer-upper that needs a high investment of time and money to bring it up to par structurally.

Don't let your business be like that fixer upper that ends up either being torn down or sold for pennies on the dollar. The good news is that, by planning ahead and taking advantage of technology, you don't have to be like the average small business owner.

"In about 2 years I was able to turn it around for successful sale at 20x investment – and the business wasn't even for sale when the buyer made an offer!"

Real life example:

In 1997, I started working with a business that was on the verge of bankruptcy. In about 2 years I was able to turn it around for successful sale at 20x investment – and the business wasn't even for sale when the buyer made an offer!

How did I do it? I developed an online store for existing products, created a new recurring revenue stream through a subscription-based service, and enhanced customer service by developing an industry-specific search engine that also opened up a platform for ad sales.

Remember, this was when Google was just a startup, many people had never heard of Amazon (but we were already selling on it), most people weren't online yet, and many highly respected professionals still thought the internet was a fad. We couldn't have imagined access to the types of online tools that you have available today.

The business wasn't a technology business, either; it was a traditional, information-based business. Developing solutions to address real problems, though, automatically created opportunities for additional income and efficiency.

"An outstanding bonus is that your business can also become more profitable and easier to run while you still own it, freeing you up to work less and start easing into your retirement before you actually sell."

If you begin preparing now, before you're ready to start trying to sell, you have time to start learning to think like a Digital Native (more on this in the next chapter). You can anticipate the systems and processes that would be worth the most to potential buyers, and implement those in your business. You may even think of new revenue streams made possible by the internet.

An outstanding bonus is that your business can also become more profitable and easier to run while you still own it, freeing you up to work less and start easing into your retirement before you actually sell.

Don't make the mistake of thinking this is a pipe dream. The value and marketability of any business can be improved with strategic use of the web.

I know you can do this! The key is to change your mindset.

Starting right now, you have to learn to think like a Digital Native. See your business through their eyes and the value will follow.

Think Like a Digital Native

You're probably wondering, "what in the heck is a Digital Native?" and "how can I think like one if I don't even know what it is?"

The term "Digital Native" was coined by Marc Prensky in 2001 and has since been widely adopted. He applied the term to the generation of people who were born or grew up during the time of widespread adoption of digital technology, as opposed to those for whom digital technology was new and had to be adopted. He refers to the previous generations of people as "Digital Immigrants," explaining:

> "The importance of the distinction is this: As Digital Immigrants learn – like all immigrants, some better than others – to adapt to their environment, they always retain, to some degree, their "accent," that is, their foot in the past. The "digital immigrant accent" can be seen in such things as turning to the Internet for information second rather than first, or in reading the manual for a program rather than assuming that the program itself will teach us to use it." (Prensky, 2001)

So what does all of this have to do with selling your business?

> *"Your job now, if you want to make your business as valuable and marketable as possible, is to start trying to think like a Digital Native."*

The more appealing you can make your business to Digital Native customers and potential buyers, the more valuable and marketable it will be. It will be recognized as being positioned for the future and ready for growth, and you'll be rewarded.

This doesn't mean the business doesn't have to keep evolving to adapt to the ever changing world of technology, but it does mean that it has a competitive advantage over other businesses that haven't begun to adapt.

The "technology gap" between Boomers and our offspring is much wider than the cultural "generation gap" between us and our own parents that was written about so much in the 60's and 70's. I believe our technology gap is actually more comparable to the generation gap between us and our grandparents. You've got to start bridging the gap.

Your job now, if you want to make your business as valuable and marketable as possible, is to start trying to think like a Digital Native.

Start looking at the web differently. Look at it as an integral part of your business and world, not a separate thing just hanging out there on its own.

It's not easy, but the more you work with people who are Digital Natives or with Digital Immigrants who have become as fluent as natives, you'll begin to transform – just as immigrants to the US in past generations did.

My husband is near the beginning of the Boomer generation and I'm at the end of Boomer and beginning of Gen X, but he's closer to a Digital Native than many people I know who are in their 40's. Why? Because our adult kids are Digital Natives and, since I've been working fully immersed in the web since 1995, the way I think is very different from some people even 15-20 years younger than me.

All of this has rubbed off on him, and it can rub off on you, too!

LISA KIPPS-BROWN

Business in the Cloud

If your head isn't spinning enough yet, now I want you to start thinking about doing business in the cloud.

What's "the cloud?" It's just another word for the internet. It means storing and accessing data on the internet rather than on your computer's hard drive, so technically you can access it from anywhere as long as you can login.

> *"Many younger people have never even installed a program on a computer, so the cloud is all they know. They're going to want any business they buy to run that way."*

You're probably already using cloud-based technology and just don't know that's what it's called. One of the most obvious examples is Facebook; your photos, videos, and posts are stored on Facebook's servers, not on your own computer. You may also be backing up your mobile phone to the cloud.

Chances are you're also already using some common cloud-based business apps like Quickbooks Online and

Google Analytics.

A major advantage of using cloud-based apps is that you can access your data from any location on any device as long as you can login; you don't have to be chained to a specific computer that has licensed software installed.

Another advantage is that, depending on how you access the service, you may not even have to update any software. If an app is installed on your device you'll need to install updates, but if you access a service through your web browser the software will always be up to date because it's installed on the provider's server.

Many younger people have never even installed a program on a computer, so the cloud is all they know. They're going to want any business they buy to run that way.

Learning to think like a Digital Native means that you need to start having your head figuratively in the cloud.

There are innumerable cloud-based software solutions (or "SaaS," meaning "Software as a Service") available now and the list is growing every day. There's no way you can ever know every one, and you don't even need to try to.

You do need to start familiarizing yourself with the types of SaaS applications (apps) that are available, though, so you can start to imagine how you may be able to use them in your business.

"When you're able to connect multiple apps together over the web to share data between them, their usefulness increases exponentially."

One app can often cover a range of functionalities, so by choosing wisely you can minimize the number you use while still having the most powerful features to help improve your business. See our Cloud Apps chart in the Resources section for examples of some apps, the various functionalities they cover, and how you may be able to use a single app for multiple purposes.

Another thing to keep in mind is that many of these SaaS apps can be connected to work together through what's called an "API" – "Application Program Interface." When you're able to connect multiple apps together over the web to share data between them, their usefulness increases exponentially. Thus, most SaaS providers develop API's that allow developers to connect their software to software from other providers.

Being able to share data between applications is great on its own, but it also gives you more flexibility for the future. For example, you can switch out one app for another for the same usage (like switching from one accounting app to another), without affecting your other apps. Connect the new app to your other existing apps via their API's and everything is back working together and sharing data.

As with the cloud, you may also already be using API's and not know it. If you have your Facebook account set up to post automatically to Twitter, the two services are communicating through their API's.

So...you're starting to think like a Digital Native and you're beginning to understand that using cloud-based apps can allow you to work more efficiently and adapt to new technology more quickly and affordably.

Now let's start to look at some of the ways you can use the web strategically in your business to do things like create new revenue streams, improve lead generation, enhance customer service, and prove marketing ROI.

Your Website

Sadly, although a website can be the most cost-effective marketing tool a business has, most still use their site as the equivalent of an online brochure. My guess is that right now yours is "set it and forget it," meaning:

- you haven't updated it in months (or even years),

- you have no online marketing strategy, and

- you have no systems in place to help you market and communicate with prospects and clients more effectively.

Since it costs 5x as much to get a new customer as it does to keep a current customer, just using your site to help nurture current customers could turn into significant sales with low marketing costs.

> *"Online strategy is a totally different animal from web design. Many people can design beautiful sites, but that doesn't mean they can help develop an online strategy that will support reaching your business goals."*

At the very least, your site should:

- be designed based on business goals and strategy,

- be developed on a CMS (Content Management System) which lets select staff with varying user permission levels login through their browser to make updates,

- integrate social media sharing and a way for visitors to subscribe to your emails, and

- be continually updated to help with search engine optimization (SEO).

For the site to contribute to growth, though, before beginning the design stage you should work on a strategic plan with someone who understands how to help you set and reach your desired business goals.

A typical web designer isn't qualified to advise on business strategy. You see, online strategy is a totally different animal from web design. Many people can design beautiful sites, but that doesn't mean they can help develop an online strategy that will support reaching business goals.

And if it isn't helping reach your business goals you're wasting money, unless your goal is to have a vanity site.

Once you do have a strategy, you need to understand how to work with a professional designer. As you wouldn't expect your doctor to write a prescription based on your self-diagnosis on WebMD, you shouldn't hire a professional web designer who will take instructions from you and just create what you say you want.

If you're going to do that, you might as well use a template-based website service like Squarespace or Wix and fill in the blanks yourself. Or hire the student down the street.

If you can't afford to work with both a web strategist and a professional designer, though, you're better off putting your budget towards the strategist. They can help you develop long-term and short-term goals and strategies, a professional plan for creating your initial site on a cost-effective template-based website service, and phases for transitioning to your own hosted website later.

The most important thing is to be working from a strategic plan, not shooting from the hip.

LISA KIPPS-BROWN

Revenue Streams

Since you already own a business you have at least one revenue stream. Believe it or not, though, there's a way that almost any business can create new revenue streams online.

> *"Your own knowledge and experience is unique to you, though, different from anyone else's in the world. That means you can more easily differentiate information or services you provide, and that differentiation is what leads to being in control of your pricing."*

While most people think only of selling traditional products online, it's often easier to make money with informational or service-based products.

Why? Because unless you have a very unique physical product, you're selling a commodity that leaves you needing to compete on price. There will always be someone who's willing to sell at a cheaper price, so you're on a downward spiral.

Your own knowledge and experience is unique to you, though, different from anyone else's in the world. That means you can more easily differentiate information or services you provide, and that differentiation is what leads to being in control of your pricing.

If you think creatively, you can begin to create new revenue streams via the web, some of which might be recurring revenue.

Recurring revenue is valuable to potential buyers because it's predictable, stable, and can be expected to continue in the future. There are different types of recurring revenue, though, and some are more valuable to buyers than others.

The highest value is from hard contracts and auto-renewing subscriptions, because they're the most highly predictable. And the auto-renewing subscription model is perfect for information and services.

> *"Almost any business can develop some type of online revenue stream, so you should be able to also. Put on your thinking cap and start brainstorming!"*

A few examples of new revenue streams you might be able to develop online include:

- **Traditional e-commerce:** The obvious is to sell your current products online, or develop new products to sell.

  If you sell your products through another site like Amazon or eBay you won't even have to have an online store developed, but you'll still need to set up all of your products (photos, description, price, shipping rates, etc.).

  There are advantages and disadvantages to selling through your own online store vs selling through a 3rd-party store, and you really should consult with an objective professional if you're not sure which you're better off doing.

- **Subscription- or membership-based content or services:** This is especially suited for products based on information, data, services, community access, or apps. Customers typically pay monthly, with an option to receive a substantial discount if they pay annually.

  These products or services can vary widely, from

business apps like Freshbooks (invoicing software) to personal services like Weight Watchers (weight loss help and community) to training sites like OS Training (educational videos and eBooks for web developers).

- **Digital products:** Downloadable products like eBooks and mobile apps. Most people who sell these include free updates for future editions or versions, giving more value to customers and making them less reluctant to buy. Done right, these products can even end up helping to sell your higher ticket products or services.

- **Coaching:** You may have experience and unique strengths that others would be willing to pay to learn from. With online coaching, you can use a combination of email courses, webinars, video instruction, and individual Skype video consulting calls. Services can be one-time or ongoing.

- **Affiliate income:** Earn money by recommending other companies' products. Products or services that are related to your own but aren't competitors are good candidates for affiliate income.

Companies that have an affiliate program will give you a specific link to include on your site. When a customer visits their site from your link, they'll know you sent the customer and you'll receive a commission on sales.

Each affiliate program has its own rules so you'll need to make sure you understand them, and keep up with any changes made to them.

A common example you've probably seen is a section of a site that has book reviews related to the business, with links to buy the books on Amazon. For example, a hardware store might link to do-it-yourself books that it recommends to its customers, or a medical office might link to various health-related books.

- **Pay-per-view access to content:** This could be anything from an article to a movie to a PDF. The customer pays a flat fee to be able to access the content for a specific period of time or number of times.

I'm sure you're used to pay-per-view movies, but

other sites like newspapers, magazines, and information sources like credit checks and background checks also use this model.

- **Live events like conferences or webinars:** You can charge ahead of time for the live event and make the recorded event available for pay-per-view for those who can't watch it live. Including a soft sell at the end to cross-sell or upsell other products also turns the conference or webinar into a sales tool.

As far as receiving payment, with affiliate sales you'll typically provide the seller your bank account number for them to deposit commissions to; alternatively, they may deposit to a PayPal account.

With the other revenue types, you'll need a method to sell via (e.g. shopping cart software, one-time payment button), and a way to accept payments online. Currently, the easiest and quickest merchant services to set up for e-commerce are PayPal and Stripe. Because they were developed specifically for the web, their API's (see the Business in the Cloud chapter) are already integrated with most shopping cart systems.

For example, all you need to set up PayPal for payment is your PayPal account email address, whereas merchant services through other providers are more complicated to set up and require API keys; often special software (called plugins) must also be developed and installed.

Since almost any business can develop some type of online revenue stream, you should be able to also. Put on your thinking cap and start brainstorming!

LISA KIPPS-BROWN

Social Media

There's one thing you need to understand: using social media isn't an option. There's a saying in our industry: "Even if you think you aren't on social media, you are." Allow me to explain with a true story that happened to a client of ours.

> *"The Fair is now actively using social media, but before they were 'using' it they were still 'on' it."*

During the week leading up to a major performer appearing at a rural Fair, a girl posted on Facebook that tickets were sold out for the performance. This was untrue, but because the Fair wasn't using social media they couldn't get out in front of it.

Running ads in a newspaper couldn't combat a time-sensitive problem like that. Sadly, ticket sales were poor all because ONE PERSON put out incorrect information and the Fair was unable to respond effectively.

The Fair is now actively using social media, but before they were "using" it they were still "on" it. I hope you'll learn from their misfortune.

Don't feel like you need to do everything, though! Choose the platforms that fit your type of business, your target market, and your personality, and go with those. If you're totally new to social media, I recommend starting with one platform and getting used to it before trying to expand. Otherwise you'll be like the person who tries to start a new diet and a new exercise program at the same time, and you'll fall off the wagon after about a week.

Currently, the platforms you may be most likely to use include Facebook, Twitter, Instagram, Pinterest, YouTube, SlideShare, and LinkedIn.

Regardless of which platforms you use, though, you must develop goals, strategy, and a plan if you expect to see results.

Marketing and Sales

Using the web effectively in marketing and sales is one of the absolute best ways you can build long term value. Proper integration and execution of the right systems can help boost sales, generate qualified leads, and fill your pipeline. You can also prove ROI of marketing campaigns to help you spend your marketing dollars more wisely, possibly resulting in substantial savings.

Facebook Messenger ads and chatbots

Ignore this huge new opportunity at your own peril! According to Facebook's current stats (Facebook, 2017):

- 2 Billion messages are sent between people and businesses each month, including both automated and people-initiated,

- 53% of people say they're more likely to do business with a business they can message, and

- 100,000 monthly active bots, and counting, are on the Messenger platform.

More than a billion people currently use Facebook Messenger to communicate and the number will continue to grow. It's only natural that it's the perfect place to communicate with prospects and interact with customers, and users love it because they're in full control of whether a business can contact them through Messenger. And unlike text messaging, Messenger is free for you to use! *(note: ads aren't free)*

A true example of Messenger being used in marketing:

A young woman in Austin saw a billboard for a new apartment complex being built, so she went to the company's Facebook page and contacted them through their "Message Us" button. They responded almost instantly (you can also have an automated reply for those times that you can't be online, like in the middle of the night).

Every step of her communication with the company was done through Facebook Messenger (except the actual tour) – including signing the lease agreement! Think of the convenience and time savings to both the customer and the company. And all from a free service.

It's just a fact that as people become more immersed in digital, they want to be able to communicate and transact business digitally rather than in-person, and Facebook Messenger is a great way for businesses to make the transition.

Facebook just opened up the opportunity to integrate ads with Messenger in November, 2016, and the response has been huge.

There are currently 2 kinds of Messenger ads: destination ads and sponsored messages.

1. Destination ads display in a user's Facebook newsfeed like other ads, but when someone clicks the ad, a message to your Facebook page opens in Facebook Messenger so they can begin a conversation. The conversation can be an actual person replying, or it can be a chatbot – an automated reply system you've set up (see below) – and the user can move from a chatbot into a personal conversation.

2. Sponsored messages are broadcasts to multiple people, more like an email list. You can only send them to people who've messaged your page in the past, and people can unsubscribe from your messages at any time.

What's a Messenger chatbot?

A chatbot is an automated reply system that can send text, images, links and call-to-action (CTA) buttons through Facebook Messenger. They can be used for things like getting answers to common questions, making a restaurant reservation, seeing the most recent listings for a real estate broker, or finding out the daily specials for a restaurant.

You can even accept payments directly in Messenger, without the customer having to leave to go to your website!

The possibilities are limited only by your imagination and the use is sure to skyrocket. Those who are early adopters of the technology will have a big leg up on competitors.

To view samples of how you can use Messenger chatbots, visit our Facebook page (username glerincreates), click the "Send Message" button, and type the word "SAMPLES" in the composer.

Email Marketing

If you're already using any of the tools in this section, my bet is on email marketing. I'm also betting big that you're using it wrong.

Let me guess: every once in a while, you send an email blast out to everyone on your list. The same exact message to each recipient.

Just like the mass mailers you get in snail mail, your email blasts go straight into most people's trash – but worse, they also cause people to unsubscribe from your list.

Every day businesses all over the world send irrelevant emails to people who have asked to be added to their email lists. That's not only a waste, but a breach of the trust you had to earn to even get a person on your list. Sending out email blasts is today's equivalent of throwing everything against the wall in the hopes that something sticks. It's also lazy and rude.

The sad thing is that it's so easy to send emails that people actually look forward to getting, which nets you high open and click-through rates and helps nurture your list. It's crazy that marketers can't understand that simply sending information to the people who are interested in receiving it is the absolute best way to grow a business.

Consider data like:

- Segmented email campaigns have a 14.31% higher open rate than non-segmented campaigns. (Mailchimp, 2017)

- Triggered emails have a 624% higher conversion rate than email blasts, resulting from a 381% higher click rate and 180% higher post-click conversion rate. (VentureBeat, 2016)

Don't get smug if you think you're already segmenting, though. Most who claim to segment their lists are only segmenting by demographics. Advanced tactics like segmenting by purchase history, click-through rates, how long a person watched a video, type and amount of purchase, and online purchase history are much more successful. How can you do that, though?

The answer is automated email segmentation.

By using the right email marketing system, you can automate the entire list segmentation process.

You can set up rules to automatically add and remove contacts to/from specific lists based on actions they take. Things like downloading a PDF, filling out a form, or visiting a specific page on your website can automatically assign a person to a specific list.

And you don't have to email everyone on a list at one time. The rules you set up can email a person *when and if they meet the criteria.*

Think about it in everyday terms. You could do things like automatically email everyone who:

- signed up for a Model Home tour,

- didn't open a certain email, or

- owns a car that's coming due for a service date.

An example of information the right people would love to get?

If you're a home health care company, you could send a series of educational emails to someone who has downloaded a PDF about Alzheimer's caregiving. As my mother's caregiver for the final years of her life, I would have been so grateful for any information that might have helped me better help her – or helped me not feel like I was losing my own mind.

So many things are helpful to know: how to get them to eat when they don't want to, what to say and not say when they don't know who you are, how to help other people understand the loved one's disease.

You can see where the right person would welcome the emails in this example.

There's plenty of information your own business can share, too. Depending on the type of business you're in, it could be helpful tips and reminders, current developments in your industry, healthy recipes, sales and promotions – *whatever would be valued and appreciated by the people in a particular segmented list.*

Marketing Automation

Website visitors now prefer to educate themselves about products and companies as much as possible, and only have contact with the company when they're near the bottom of the funnel – ready to convert.

Using marketing automation allows you to attract and

nurture leads at their preferred pace, stay front of mind, give them the right content at the right time in the buyer's journey, and know when they're ready for contact.

A few of the things you can do include:

- Adapt your website content to each website visitor based on their behavior, for a more personal web experience. The example you're probably familiar with is Amazon's product recommendations, but it can be done in any industry.

- Automatically send personalized emails to customers or leads based on what they do on your site – things like abandoning a shopping cart, downloading a specific file, or even visiting an important page.

- Create landing pages and traffic funnels that nurture very targeted prospects through the sales process from awareness to conversion.

- Create forms that automatically update a contact's information in your Customer

Relationship Management (CRM) system.

- Receive a text or email when an important person visits your site, or visits a specific page on your site.

- Identify anonymous site visitors to help identify more leads.

- Set up lead scoring to award points to leads as they do things like move through your sales funnel, visit specific pages, or interact with emails you send.

- When a lead reaches a certain score, automatically assign them to a member of your sales team. This lets your team stop wasting time working unqualified leads and concentrate on those most likely to buy.

- Attribute leads and customers to different marketing campaigns based on rules you set.

- Track marketing campaigns and measure ROI so you'll know what is and isn't working in your marketing, allowing you to adapt to save money and increase sales.

- Even use call tracking to correlate phone calls with specific website visitors, to provide better customer service and more in-depth data.

The marketing automation apps that we recommend are SharpSpring and Drip. SharpSpring is the ultimate and includes a full CRM, a landing page generator, the ability to track marketing campaign ROI, and sales tools like assigning leads to sales team members, tracking opportunities through the pipeline, and projecting revenues. If you've heard of HubSpot, SharpSpring is similar but is a fraction of the cost and works with any content management system, whereas your website has to be developed on HubSpot to access all of its features.

Blogging

When a lot of people think of blogging, they think of someone sitting in their basement in pajamas, writing in the middle of the night. Wrong!

It's actually a great way to promote your business, and even to generate more revenue either through increased sales due to raised awareness or revenues from paid sponsorships of the blog.

In case you don't know, a blog just refers to a system that

displays content that's regularly added to a site and lists it by date – usually from newest to oldest. A blog system includes tags (a way to categorize content by keyword), subscriptions (so people can opt in to be notified when you have a new post), comments (to allow readers to comment on a post and interact with you), and social media integration (to make it easy for people to share your content on social media).

The system can be installed within your own site or may already be built into the content management system that your website runs on.

Blogs are popular in marketing because they're a way for you to demonstrate expertise and can also help your search engine ranking:

- The more content you have on your site, the more content search engines can index (think of it like raffle tickets, the more tickets you have the more chances you have to be drawn).

- Because blog posts are usually about a focused topic, they're typically naturally keyword-rich without being written in an awkward manner.

- As search engines have to compete more with social media, they're always looking for fresh, new content. Regularly adding new content to your site will cause search engines to come back more frequently to crawl your site. As with food, fresh sells!

- When related sites link to your blog posts, it signals to search engines that you're an authority on your topic, further boosting your search ranking.

Podcasting

Think of podcasting as a talk radio show, but one that listeners can subscribe to and listen to on demand.

In the early 2000's podcasting had a period of popularity that dropped off as video surged, but the past several years have seen podcasting's popularity explode. According to statistics from a study by Edison Research as reported by Jay Baer (Baer, 2017):

- 24% of Americans aged 12 or older listen to podcasts monthly.

- 15% of the total US population listen to podcasts

weekly.

That's amazing. What's with podcasts' popularity? Simple: unlike watching a video or reading, you can listen to a podcast while you're doing other things – like driving a car.

Personally, I always listen to marketing podcasts while I'm mowing the lawn. I get my strength and cardio in, get to absorb valuable content, and am also doing something productive at the same time. It's multitasking to the max and I can't consume any other kind of content that way, except music or audiobooks.

Most podcast hosts interview other people in their industry or talk in depth about a related topic, so it's a great way to demonstrate authority for both host and guest.

If you publish your podcast on a regular basis, you can build a significant following which, at the very least, translates into increased awareness of you and your product or service but may also contribute directly to sales.

Webinars

A webinar is a presentation, seminar, or workshop that's given over the internet; it's short for "web-based seminar."

It can be presented by live video or you can post recordings for people to watch on demand, or both.

There are a number of reasons that webinars are great for marketing, including:

- they give your audience a chance to feel like they're getting to know you,

- they let you demonstrate your expertise,

- you can get product feedback,

- presented correctly, they can generate qualified leads or even closed sales,

- and they can be used to train customers in how to use your product or service more effectively.

In addition to using them in marketing, you can also use webinars in the new revenue streams that you create as you transform your business. A popular application of them is in a subscription-based educational series, where you develop training videos that customers pay to be able to access.

So... you can use a webinar to help sell other webinars!

Administration & Operations

There are so many apps for various uses and each business has its own unique needs, but I'll point out a few here just to give you an idea of what's currently out there.

Accounting & Invoicing

The grandaddy of small business accounting apps is Quickbooks Online because it's been around so long. There are many new apps, though, that give Quickbooks a run for its money, especially for service-based businesses.

My favorite cloud-based app for invoicing is Freshbooks, which is browser-based and also has a mobile app. We use Quickbooks for accounting but Freshbooks for invoicing because it's so user-friendly. We just import data from Freshbooks into Quickbooks for accounting purposes.

> *"If you need to cover short-term cash flow gaps, Freshbooks also integrates with Fundbox. Fundbox is a simple way for small businesses to meet cashflow needs*

without having a bank line of credit."

Freshbooks isn't full accounting software, but lets you create professional-looking invoices that include online credit card payment support.

You can also set up repeat invoicing, send estimates that convert to invoices when accepted, track expenses to add to invoices, and send one-click snail mail invoices (we don't use this feature).

Customers also have the option of setting up automatic payment of their invoices by credit card, which gets you paid as soon as the invoice is issued. Freshbooks integrates with PayPal for accepting payment, as well as WePay. You can sign up for WePay directly within your Freshbooks account.

If you need to cover short-term cash flow gaps, Freshbooks also integrates with Fundbox to help you meet cashflow needs without having a bank line of credit. It's a service that lets you get advances on your outstanding invoices transferred directly to your banking account. You have the option of paying advances back in 12 or 24 weeks and there's no penalty for early repayment.

Human Resources

PC Magazine's Best Human Resources Management Software of 2017 Editor's Choice (PC Magazine, 2017) selected 3 apps that were rated 4.5 out of 5 for its Editor's Choice Award:

Zenefits is free, and is best for startups to SMB's. You only pay for optional add-ons, or if you use it as your employee benefits broker.

BambooHR is priced per user per month and is simple to set up and run, but benefits administration isn't very advanced.

Gusto (formerly ZenPayroll) has a monthly base fee plus a fee per employee. PC Magazine says it's "the best cloud-based payroll solution with built-in benefits administration (BA) for small to midsize businesses (SMBs) on a tight budget."

Help Desk / Customer Support

Freshdesk offers a free version and lets you customize the interface with your brand. It's not the best choice for IT ticket management, but is suitable for straight ticket management that the average small business needs.

HappyFox features self-service tools to provide solutions to common problems, and automation rules that help reduce ticket management workload. It's one of PC Magazine's Best Help Desk Software of 2017 Editor's Choice winners (PC Magazine, 2017).

Jira Service Desk integrates with Confluence, a collaboration app that's in the next section. It's the primary issue tracking tool for many Open Source software projects.

Scheduling, Communication, and Collaboration

The following is just a small sampling of the wide variety of apps available to help your business run more efficiently. Most have a free version as well as optional paid upgrades.

If you can imagine it, there's probably an app for it, but hopefully this list will help you start imagining the many possibilities for using the web to streamline your business.

> *"No matter what it is, chances are there's an app for that. And if there isn't, you've just come up with an idea for a new product to develop :)"*

Try this: make a list of the most annoying parts of running your business and look for an app to help.

Maybe it's going back and forth on email to set up meetings? Or getting new clients onboarded? Or how about email threads between multiple people that are impossible to follow? No matter what it is, chances are there's an app for that. And if there isn't, you've just come up with an idea for a new product to develop :)

Calendly is a scheduling app that lets people set appointments with you. You set up your availability preferences, and share the link or embed the calendar on your website; clients select a time and it's added to your calendar. You can create buffer times and prevent last minute meetings. Calendly also automatically detects each person's timezone so everyone is on the same page.

Facebook Messenger is great for automated or personal communications with prospects or customers. Refer back to the Marketing and Sales section for more info.

Google Drive is a file storage and synchronization service that lets your team collaborate on editing documents, spreadsheets, presentations, drawings, forms, and more. The files are saved on Google Drive, and you can also download them to your hard drive. Many other apps integrate with Drive.

Slack is a free collaboration tool that offers real-time messaging similar to text messaging, but lets you organize chats by topic. It's very popular in the tech industry, and can be used for internal communication as well as communicating with clients. It allows both group and individual messaging, including file attachments, and searching all content in your channel.

Dropbox is a secure file storage and syncing system that lets you access your files from any device. You can also share files with other users, and set their access level (e.g. whether a user is able to just view a file vs. edit it).

Skype lets you call anyone anywhere in the world for free, using your computer or mobile device. You can have video conferences with one or more people, share your screen with them, send text messages, and upload files to share with them. It's a great way to have meetings with clients and coworkers who are located in other places. We also use it for training and consulting.

Meistertask is a project and task management tool that includes features like Kanban project dashboards (virtual cards that you can drag to rearrange), time tracking, project workflow, mind maps, and real-time reporting.

Buffer is an app that lets you manage multiple social media accounts and schedule posts. You can also add team members to your Buffer account so multiple people can contribute to your social media accounts.

Evernote lets you create notes that can be anything from formatted text to a full web page, a voice memo, or photo. You can attach files to notes, and tag, edit, comment on, and search notes. Since it includes OCR (Optical Character Recognition), you can even search text in uploaded images like business cards.

Confluence lets team members collaborate, discuss work, record decisions, and comment on documents, providing context and history of a project and the team.

Putting it All Together

I'm sure your head really is spinning by now and you're overwhelmed. You probably even feel like it's impossible to do all of this stuff, so why even try? For your future, that's why.

> *"One thing is for sure: by developing and executing a roadmap to modernize your business, you'll be better off even before you try to sell it."*

I want to stress that, although I covered quite a bit of information in this book, you don't need to learn it all yourself, do it all on your own, or do it all at once. Surround yourself with people who understand digital to improve your results, but make sure they're qualified and don't be fooled by posers.

Don't get your advice from peers who happen to have read an article and all of a sudden they're an expert because they know some new words. They're like the new business college graduate with book knowledge and no experience in the real world who thinks they know everything.

I've also seen too many business owners hoodwinked by unqualified new hires who BS'ed their way into a job. Throwing around words you don't understand doesn't mean they know what they're talking about. You need an experienced digital translator who can ask the right questions to decipher whether the person is actually qualified.

Here are some things you can do to help develop your plan, but pace yourself:

1. Make notes of your competitive strengths and weaknesses. Think about what would probably be attractive to both customers and potential buyers, as well as things that may be seen as negative.

2. Make a list of your competitors, along with their strengths and weaknesses.

3. Document your Unique Selling Proposition (USP), why someone should buy from you instead of your competitors.

4. Work with a professional to do an honest review of your entire website – not just what it looks like, but more importantly, concentrate on the

content, navigational structure, user-friendliness, search engine results, etc.

5. Document your marketing and sales processes and systems, and your sales funnels. Include everyone who works in these areas and what they do as well as the names of any systems you're already using, such as email marketing or CRM, and how you're using them.

6. Document any social media platforms you're using, current level of results (e.g. how many followers, shares, etc.), goals, and strategies. List any other platforms you think you should begin to use.

7. Use the information from the preceding steps to help develop an overall Project Roadmap for things you should do to modernize and improve your business. The roadmap should cover where you are, where you want to go, and how you plan to get there.

I recommend the first steps in your plan be things you can do relatively easily. This will boost your confidence and give you the satisfaction of progress.

It's common for a roadmap to cover anywhere from 6 months to 2 years, depending on where your business is at. Remember, though, the roadmap needs to be a living plan that can be adapted if things change.

8. Use your roadmap to begin to transform your business. Staff buy-in is important, so make sure to let them know the importance of what you're doing and how it can help them by making their jobs easier or by making the business more profitable. They may even have some great ideas. D*on't tell them you're doing it to prepare for sale! Keep this quiet until you're ready for people to know.*

9. As your roadmap is progressing, take time to notice the differences in your business. Maybe you're making more money, maybe staff is happier, maybe there are less customer complaints, maybe you're just able to work fewer hours because you're not trying to do it all yourself! Whatever it is, savor the progress.

One thing is for sure: by developing and executing a roadmap to modernize your business, you'll be better off even before you try to sell it.

If you would like to share your journey with me, please feel free to email me at lisa@glerin.com. I'd love to know how things are working out for you, and may even be able to use you in a case study to help you get some added publicity.

Don't be afraid to ask for help if you need it. This is about your future, and about profiting as much as possible from all of the work you've already put into your business over the years.

Here's to being able to retire and enjoy the fruits of your labor when you're ready to make that move to cash out!

Glossary

Application Program Interface (API) - a set of routines, protocols, and tools for building software applications that specifies how software should interact.

Affiliate Marketing - earning a commission by promoting other companies' products.

App – short for "application," it can refer to mobile apps or web apps (those that run in a web browser).

Blog – a regularly updated website or section of a website; articles ("posts") are usually written informally and displayed by date added, newest to oldest.

Call-to-action (CTA) – a button or words that urge the user to take action, like "buy now," "click to download," and "read more."

Chatbot - an automated reply system that can send text, images, links, call-to-action (CTA) buttons, and other content through apps like Facebook Messenger.

Cloud – the internet and the network of servers that make it up.

Coaching – helping someone improve their performance

in an area in which you're an expert.

Content Management System (CMS) – a computer application that supports the creation and editing of website content by multiple collaborating users.

Customer (or Client) Relationship Management (CRM) System – software used to manage and analyze customer interactions and data throughout the customer lifecycle. A CRM is used to help improve customer relationships, and generate leads to drive sales growth.

Digital Immigrant – the generations of people for whom digital technology was new and had to be adopted.

Digital Native – the generation of people who were born or grew up during the time of widespread adoption of digital technology.

Digital Product - intangible products that exist in digital form, e.g. software, MP3 music files, eBooks.

Domain Name – an address where your site can be found online, ending with extensions like .com, .org, .gov. Domain names have to be registered; while a name's registration is active, the registrant owns the right to use the name but doesn't own the name itself.

E-commerce – the process of selling products or services online.

Email Marketing – sending a commercial message to a group of people using email. Ideally, email marketing should be done through an email marketing system rather than your regular email software. The system allows you to send a email to each person on a list without other recipients being cc'ed.

Landing Page – can refer to any web page that a visitor can "land on," but usually used to refer to a page that's been developed separately from your website and has a single goal or objective – e.g. to get people to sign up for your email list or to sell a product. Many people refer to a landing page as a "sales page."

Marketing Automation – software that automates repetitive tasks to help businesses communicate with customers and prospects more effectively and marketers work more efficiently.

Membership-based site – a website that requires a user to create an account and login in order to use it; it can be paid or free, or a hybrid.

Mind Map – a diagram to visually organize information, showing relationships between pieces and the whole. Mind mapping software allows the user to create a mind map digitally (using a computer) rather than on paper.

Open Source – software with source code that's freely available and can be modified and redistributed.

Pay-per-view – a type of product that a customer pays to access on demand (vs. on a predetermined schedule). Views may be limited by number of times or period of time.

Platform – a framework that software applications run on.

Podcast – a themed, episodic series of digital audio files that listeners can subscribe to and listen to on demand using their computer or mobile device.

Project Roadmap – a high-level view of a project's goals and deliverables presented on a timeline. It's a simple story of the project, versus the project plan which is where details are fleshed out.

Revenue Stream – a form of revenue coming into a company from a specific activity over a period of time.

Sales Funnel – the buying process that a business leads customers through when purchasing products or services.

Social Media Marketing – the process of using social networking websites to increase brand awareness or promote particular products or services.

Subscription-based site – a website that users pay to access for a given period of time, usually monthly or annually. They typically offer some type of information or service.

Target Market – a particular group of consumers that a product or service is aimed at.

Traffic Funnel – the ideal journey a customer takes to reach a website and navigate site contents in the process of converting to a sale.

Unique Selling Proposition (USP) – also known as Unique Selling Point, it's the one thing that truly differentiates a company or product from its competitors.

URL – Uniform Resource Locator, it's the address or link for a particular web page. For example, glerin.com is our domain name and glerin.com/blog is the URL for our blog.

Webinar – a web-based seminar that lets people from multiple locations see and hear a presenter and ask questions. People who can't attend a live webinar can usually view a recording of it, but they won't be able to ask questions.

Resources

Books

Boomer Cashout digital versions will be updated periodically and available online for free to all previous buyers at www.glerin.com/boomer-cashout.

The Exit Planning Institute:

exit-planning-institute.org/resources/online-store/books

- *Walking to Destiny:* 11 Actions An Owner *MUST Take to Rapidly Grow Value & Unlock Wealth* - Christopher M. Snider, CEPA, CEO

- *The Master Plan Exit Strategy For Successful Business Owners* - Peter. G. Christman, foreword by Christopher M. Snider

- *$10 Trillion Opportunity* – *Designing Successful Exit Strategies for Middle Market Business Owners* – Richard E. Jackim and Peter. G. Christman

- *Every Family's Business* – Thomas William Deans, PhD

Buy-Sell Agreements for Closely Held and Family

Business Owners – Z. Christopher Mercer, ASA, CFA, ABAR

Buy-Sell Agreements for Baby Boomer Business Owners (The Baby Boomer Business Owner Transition Guide Series) - Z. Christopher Mercer, ASA, CFA, ABAR

Cashing Out of Your Business – Your Last Great Deal – Kathleen Richardson-Mauro, CFP, CM&AA, CBEC and Jane Johnson, CPA, CBEC, CM&AA, FBA

For Business Owners

Free Resources & Tools –

www.glerin.com/free-resources-tools

Cloud Apps Chart - www.glerin.com/apps-chart

Business Transition Academy – www.btaplans.com - BTA assists owners of privately held companies in making key transition decisions that impact their future as well as the future of their businesses, families, and employees.

Small Business Administration Plan Your Exit -

sba.gov/managing-business/closing-down-your-business/plan-your-exit

For Exit Planners

Exit Planning Institute – exit-planning-institute.org – Offeror of the Certified Exit Planning Advisor (CEPA) designation. Education, networking, professional development, and tools for exit planning professionals around the world.

Exit Planning Conference –

exitplanningconference.com - Get inside the mind of the owner and emerge with a deeper understanding of how to engage middle market business owners, trigger action, and produce results.

Sources

Baer, Jay. (n.d.). *The 11 Critical Podcast Statistics of 2017*. Retrieved May 15, 2017 from http://www.convinceandconvert.com/podcast-research/the-11-critical-podcast-statistics-of-2017.

Facebook. (n.d.). *Messenger Bots for Business and Developers.* Retrieved May 15, 2017, from https://messenger.fb.com.

Mailchimp. (Updated February 1, 2017). *Effects of List Segmentation on Email Marketing Stats.* Retrieved May 15, 2017, from https://mailchimp.com/resources/research/effects-of-list-segmentation-on-email-marketing-stats.

PC Magazine. (April 3, 2017). *The Best Helpdesk Software of 2017*. Retrieved May 15, 2017, from http://www.pcmag.com/article2/0,2817,2489457,00.asp.

PC Magazine. (April 3, 2017). *The Best Human Resources Management Software of 2017*. Retrieved May 15, 2017, from http://www.pcmag.com/article2/0,2817,2492792,00.asp.

Prensky, Marc. (2001). "Digital Natives, Digital

Immigrants Part 1", *On the Horizon*, Vol. 9 Issue: 5, pp.1-6, doi: 10.1108/10748120110424816. Permalink: http://dx.doi.org/10.1108/10748120110424816

VentureBeat. (October 14, 2016). *Study shows triggered push notifications are 2,770% better than batch messages*. Retrieved May 15, 2017 from https://venturebeat.com/2016/10/14/study-shows-triggered-push-notifications-are-2770-better-than-batch-messages

About the Author

Lisa Kipps-Brown, Business Reimagineer and Opportunity Miner, provides expert web and marketing strategy with no gobbledygook. She specializes in helping entrepreneurs transform their business model and increase their company's market value using the web and strategic partnerships.

Her 30 years of entrepreneurial and 25 years of Internet business experience provide a foundation of expertise that's unmatched.

Since starting her web and marketing strategy firm in 1996, she's been a pioneer in adapting businesses to compete using the ever-changing web in ways that blend with the physical world.

Lisa approaches projects in a holistic way. Starting with the client's problems and goals, she works outward to s that address multiple pain points rather s.

Her achievements are diverse, ranging from transforming a private company facing bankruptcy into one that sold at 20 times investment in less than 2 years, to creating groundbreaking initiatives for a 10-county economic development region that have enabled it to support, promote, and train its entrepreneurial community.

LinkedIn: @lisakippsbrown
Twitter: @lisakippsbrown
Facebook: @lisakippsbrown.reimagineer
Instagram: @lisakippsbrown
Blog: lisakippsbrown.com/blog